Family Law Issues in Agriculture

Cari B. Rincker, Esq.

By Cari B. Rincker, Esq.

DEDICATION

To my parents, who have given me both roots and wings.

And to my grandparents, who showed me the value of hard work and the simple pleasures of farm life.

- Cari B. Rincker, Esq.

INTRODUCTION

I never thought that I would be a divorce lawyer. After all, my parents have been married for over four decades and I grew up watching my grandparents hold hands and singing "Have a told you lately that I love you." The truth is, I fell into family law.

I started my law practice out of a studio apartment on the Upper East Side in the most densely populated city in the United States. I had no clients, no money, but a lot of heart and hustle. In efforts to pay rent, I practiced "door law" taking whatever cases came through the door. Invariably, I had my first divorce case that came across my desk.

I was fortunate to have found a good mentor to help hand-hold me through my first, second, third, and even fourth divorce case. During this time, I grew a strong passion for helping people navigate through some of the darkest, most stressful times in their life. I went to law school because I wanted to help people but I wasn't sure how. As the book goes to print, I have practiced family law for over a decade. With each case and each family came new lessons about people and how to help them navigate this transition in their life.

I am a farm girl. I grew up baling hay and showing cattle through 4-H and FFA in Shelbyville, Illinois. I have advanced degrees in animal science and a love for the agriculture industry and the people who grow our food. I love seeing multi-generational farm families and feel strongly about farm succession planning to help families transition their farm, ranch, or agribusiness to the next generation. Divorce, however, is one of the Big D's that families need to consider and plan for along with destruction and death.

I am not passionate about divorce but I am passionate about helping people. Frankly, divorce, separations, and break-ups are a part of life. I feel strongly that people do not have to let divorce ruin their lives, their family, or their ability to have wealth and security.

I hope this book arms the readers with general information that they can use to help guide them through this chapter alongside a learned family law attorney who understands agriculture and other professionals who may help guide you, such as mediators, therapists, accountants, financial advisors, appraisers, etc.

"Accept what is, let go of what was, and have faith in what will be." – Sonia Ricotti

By Cari B. Rincker, Esq.

TABLE OF CONTENTS

By Cari B. Rincker, Esq.

ACKNOWLEDGEMENTS

Proofreading: Jill Ewing and Kat Bork
Assistance with Editing: National Agriculture Law Center
Headshot Photographer: CB Photography
Book Cover Design: Ranch House Designs, Inc.

Cari Rincker is a partner of the National Agricultural Law Center (www.nationalaglawcenter.org) at the University of Arkansas System Division of Agriculture, which serves as the nation's leading source of agricultural and food law research and information. This material is provided as part of that partnership and is based upon work supported by the National Agricultural Library, Agricultural Research Service, U.S. Department of Agriculture.

CHAPTER 1

NUPTIAL AGREEMENTS

Prenuptial agreements are oftentimes viewed as taboo; instead, farmers, ranchers, agribusiness owners, and food entrepreneurs should view prenuptial agreements like an insurance policy for a marriage. Nobody gets on an airplane thinking that it is going to crash, but you still go over the safety instructions. A prenuptial agreement simply notes the safety instructions in case the marriage terminates for whatever reason.

It is a common misconception that prenuptial agreements are only for the rich and famous; in fact, almost anyone entering a marriage can benefit from a prenuptial agreement. It allows the parties to put the law into their own hands and "create their own rules" for the division of property and other ancillary economic issues with a divorce or separation. Prenuptial agreements should be viewed an empowering exercise, allowing the couple to have their own autonomy to dictate their own rules.

Arguably, the exercise of preparing and negotiating a prenuptial agreement requires couples to have tough conversations that may strengthen their bond. Both parties are forced to become financially naked and share intimate details of his/her finances prior to the wedding date; this alone can be a healthy exercise for most couples as each party must attach a Schedule of Assets and Debts to the prenuptial agreement. In some instances, parties may decide to exchange tax returns or limited financial documentation to support the figures. Clarity as to the financial picture of the soon-to-be spouse is oftentimes gained during this process.

Prenuptial agreements are typically enforced in most states if (1) both sides are represented by separate counsel, (2) the terms are fair and reasonable, and (3) there was not any duress or undue influence (i.e., signed voluntarily). Furthermore, the prenuptial agreement should be properly signed and executed in accordance with state law.

Although the agreement should be specially tailored for each individual family, the purpose of this chapter is to discuss the major issues with prenuptial agreements, as they apply to the food and agriculture industry. Issues that cannot be discussed in the prenuptial agreement include provisions regarding children (except for religion in some states). Additionally, cheating clauses and lifestyle clauses (i.e., promises not to smoke or drink) are typically not enforceable.

IDENTIFICATION OF SEPARATE AND MARITAL PROPERTY

Property in a marriage fits into one of three buckets: *two separate (or nonmarital)* property buckets and the *marital property* bucket.

Spouse 1 Bucket	Marital Bucket	Spouse 2 Bucket

Prenuptial agreements always identify what is in each party's separate property bucket and what is in the marital bucket. Parties can decide to deviate from the law in this area on how they decide what fits in the three buckets. For example, property in joint name or property gifted to the parties in joint name are clearly marital property, but here are some other areas to consider:

PROPERTY AND DEBT PRIOR TO THE MARRIAGE

Generally speaking, all property acquired prior to the marriage is considered separate property. Prenuptial agreements will attach a Schedule of Assets and Debts for each party and usually, but not always, the prenuptial agreement will note that it is that person's responsibility. With a minority of prenuptial agreements, couples put certain accounts or property into the marital bucket.

Furthermore, what if one person enters the marriage with

substantial student loans or other debts? The prenuptial agreement can include provisions if the other party helps pay down this separate debt during the marriage.

BUSINESS INTERESTS

With farmers, ranchers, agribusiness owners, and food entrepreneurs, this is perhaps the most important issue to focus on. In the laws in most states, businesses formed during the marriage are considered marital property. If the business was already in existence on the wedding day, then the appreciation of the business during the marriage can be considered marital property if the other spouse was either actively or inactively involved in the business itself. To illustrate, if Susie married Farmer Sam and the farm was owned in his individual name, but Susie helped him for decades around the farm, then the court would look at her efforts and the appreciation of the farm enterprise during the marriage thanks, in part, to her involvement at home or in the farm business.

Therefore, the prenuptial agreement should clearly note whether any present *or future* businesses will fit in a separate or the marital bucket. There can be negotiation with this issue, especially for the non-titled spouse, so it is important that couples are on the same page. Parties can negotiate a clean walk away from one spouse, a vesting schedule in accordance with the years of marriage (i.e., after X years the spouse will own Y percentage of the business).

INCOME

Income itself is typically a negotiated issue with a prenuptial agreement. *By default in most states, income from wherever derived is considered marital property.* Even if a spouse puts monies in an individual account, said income is still considered marital. This is an important point for agriculture couples to be on the same page and they should ask themselves how they view each other's income and how they plan to manage their finances as a married couple.

The prenuptial agreement should not only address whether income as an employee and independent contractor income is separate or marital, but it should also clearly identify how income derived from businesses, whether in salary, draw, or profits, is handled. With business owners, such as farmers and ranchers, this is a hot issue as so much of the monies generated from food and agriculture operations are put back into the business itself. Spouses waiving his or her rights to the business itself may need safeguards on income, requiring that the farm business pay the spouse a reasonable salary and that income be considered marital.

RETIREMENT AND INVESTMENT ACCOUNTS

Retirement devices, including pensions and annuities, and investment accounts, including stocks and bonds, are an important topic to discuss with prenuptial agreements. This can be an emotional topic and oftentimes, but not always, goes hand-in-hand with how the couple views income. Self-employed farmers, ranchers, and agribusiness owners have a lot of control over what monies are put into retirement and investment devices.

DOWN PAYMENTS AND CONTRIBUTIONS TO REAL PROPERTY

The law varies in this area from state-to-state, but couples entering into a prenuptial agreement can make their own rules. It is not unusual for the prenuptial agreement to note that if either party uses his or her separate property for a down payment on real estate, then that person will receive a dollar-for-dollar credit back if the marriage is dissolved.

> *Example: Farmer Jane and John live together in a farmstead adjacent to John's family. The neighbor's farm comes up for sale. John takes $50,000 from his premarital wealth to use for the down payment for the $500,000 farm. Depending on how the prenuptial agreement is drafted, the new farm may be marital property and is jointly titled. If the couple dissolves their marriage 20 years later, John would receive back his $50,000 down payment and the couple would split the equity 50/50 (or by whatever rules the prenuptial agreement dictates).*

That being said, some prenuptial agreements take this concept one step further. In the below example, not only would John receive his dollar-for-dollar credit back, but he too would receive appreciation on that separate property down payment.

To keep the math simple, this $500,000 farm is now worth $1 million 20 years later and the parties have a $100,000 mortgage at the date of separation (i.e., whatever operative event language used in the prenuptial agreement). John would receive a $100,000 separate property credit (i.e., $50,000 plus 100% appreciation). The parties would then split the remaining equity of the farm after the payment of the mortgage equally ($400,000 each) or in accordance with the terms of the prenuptial agreement.

GIFTS AND INHERITANCES

The general rule is that gifts and inheritances during the marriage are considered separate property. Prenuptial agreements will typically note that gifts in an individual name are considered separate property, but gifts in joint name, including wedding and engagement gifts, are considered marital property.

DISTRIBUTION OF MARITAL PROPERTY

The next issue usually, but not always, discussed in the prenuptial agreement is how the marital bucket will be divided in a divorce action. There are three options here:

1. Silence on the issue or defaulting to the law;
2. Splitting the marital bucket equally (50/50); or
3. Make your own rules.

This area can be as simple or complicated as the couple desires. Perhaps the farm couple wants all assets to be divided equally (50/50), but then has a certain vesting scheduling in accordance with the length of the marriage for the farm business and its assets.

Example: Farmer Jane marries Farmer Fred, who comes from a multi-generational farm family. Farmer Fred owns a 20% interest in the family farm, which is identified as non-marital property in the prenuptial agreement. The couple agrees on a chart where, based on the number of years of marriage, Farmer Jane would acquire an ownership interest in the family farm. After a 25 year marriage, she will have a 50% interest of the 20% shares (i.e., 10% ownership interest) based on her sweat equity and efforts during the marriage. The couple agreed, for illustration purposes, on the following vesting schedule:

Length of Marriage	Husband's Ownership Interest	Wife's Ownership Interest
5 years	90%	10%
10 years	80%	20%
15 years	70%	30%
20 years	60%	40%
25 years	50%	50%

Furthermore, this section of the prenuptial agreement can include provisions relating to valuation of any farm, ranch, agribusiness, or food company. For example, it may specifically note that the parties will hire an agreed-upon business valuator to value the company(ies) at two points of time -- (1) date of the marriage and (2) date of separation -- splitting the costs of same on an equal or *pro rata* (based on income) basis. The prenuptial agreement can then provide for the scenario if they aren't able to agree on a business valuator (e.g. each party hires their own valuator and averages the two).

SPOUSAL MAINTENANCE

Spousal maintenance is *almost always* discussed in a prenuptial agreement in one shape or form. Here again there are three options:

1. Silence or follow the law in that state;
2. Waiver (or partial-waiver); or
3. Make your own rules.

Parties should be cautious to waive their right to support. Even though a party may be healthy and employed at the time of signing the prenuptial agreement, it may not always be the case. If one or both parties choose to waive their right of support, they should consider a limited exception if they are disabled and no longer employable or are out of the workforce for whatever reason for X number of years.

For couples that wish to "make their own rules," they should begin with the law in that state and determine the spousal maintenance calculations at that snapshot in time. Then the couple should consider how they wish to deviate from that formula in any way. For example, there can be income caps or a set formula for the number of years of maintenance. Couples may determine support based on the years of marriage. The sky is the limit on how the rules can be determined. What is important here is that the parties understand the inherent risks with these provisions in either direction.

ESTATE RIGHTS

People oftentimes assume that all provisions in a prenuptial agreement are only applicable if you get divorced; estate rights are an example of provisions that come into play, even if the couple decides to never divorce. Estate rights are usually, but not always, discussed in the prenuptial agreement.

As a general rule in most states, you cannot disinherit your spouse. Your spouse will be entitled to a certain percentage of your estate, even if you do not include any provision in your Last Will and Testament for this person. With estate rights, the parties again have three options:

1. Silence or follow the law in that state;
2. Waiver; or
3. Make your own rules.

Waivers are more typical with parties with substantial premarital wealth or second/third/fourth marriages, especially when there are children of prior relationships that may receive the inheritance. Parties are free to give what they wish to their spouse in their Last Will and Testament, but the law's "security blanket" disappears. *Thus, parties wishing to waive their right of inheritance in a prenuptial agreement should do so cautiously.* People can change their Last Will and Testament on their death bed and the law will no longer protect the other spouse.

Couples that decide to make their own rules may come up with their own minimum guaranteed award in accordance with the years of marriage or contribution to the estate. There can be promises about bequeathing certain property. If the prenuptial agreement conflicts with the Last Will and Testament, then the prenuptial agreement will take precedence.

As a caveat, a party has the right to inherit from the other's estate even while the divorce is pending. It is recommended in most cases that the prenuptial agreement note a waiver of estate rights upon separation or the operative event in the agreement.

PROMISES DURING MARRIAGE

This is another example of provisions in the prenuptial agreement that are applicable even if the couple never divorces. This can include provisions regarding insurance (life, disability, or long-term care) or access to money.

If there is a waiver of estate rights as discussed above, financial security can be given to the other party with a promise to maintain life insurance to a certain amount. There could also be a promise to maintain life insurance to pay for any marital debt. Parties marrying farmers or those in other professions that are more physical could consider promises for disability insurance; similarly, parties who have health issues or are older may wish to promise to maintain long-term care insurance.

Access to money or the promise to put X% of income in a joint account is an issue for some families. The couple should discuss how they wish to manage finances. This provision is rarely included in prenuptial agreements but can be added for couples that wish to have that structure.

Lifestyle clauses with promises not to smoke/drink, exercise each day, maintain a certain weight, go on a weekly date night, participate in couples counseling, help doing chores on the farm, or bring you lemonade in the field, etc. are usually not enforceable. Similarly, cheating clauses can be problematic and should be avoided.

BREAK-UP PROCEDURES

"Breaking up is hard to do..." but terms in the prenuptial agreement can help by providing some clear structure. Some couples do not wish to include these provisions, while others want the break-up instructions laid out. For example, there can be clauses on who will move out of the marital residence if the property is titled in the name of only one party or the procedures for buying out the other party if the marital residence is owned in joint name. Procedures for putting the marital residence up for sale, including an agreed-upon choice of a real estate broker, can also be spelled out.

Parties may also wish to include an Alternative Dispute Resolution ("ADR") clause (e.g., mediation for economic issues) or promise to use a collaborative divorce process in the case of separation.

MISCELLANEOUS TERMS

This includes a choice of law provision. Oftentimes, couples request a confidentiality clause so that terms of the prenuptial agreement are required to stay private, but for the exception of financial advisors, lawyers, and immediate family members.

Although you can see "sunset provisions" in any area of prenuptial agreement, the couple may choose to have an overarching sunset provision noting that the prenuptial agreement itself is not valid after they have been married for X number of years or if X event takes place.

CONCLUSION

The prenuptial agreement process can be empowering for parties and requires the couple to have those tough conversations. This is an important liability protection device for farmers, ranchers, agribusiness owners, and food entrepreneurs because, if a divorce occurs, the parties understand the rules because they created them. *Divorce is one of the Big D's along with destruction and death that can harm multigenerational food and agriculture businesses.* Every farm and ranch should have a business and succession plan, there too should be a game plan if relationships dissolve. Prenuptial agreements can be a helpful insurance policy for those involved in any segment of the food and agriculture industry and set forth a clear roadmap for both parties.

For more information:

Chris Zoller and Davis Marrison, "Is a Prenuptial Agreement Right for Your Fam Business?" April 11, 2018 at
https://ohioline.osu.edu/factsheet/anr-51

Sara Schafer, "How Prenuptial Agreements Protect Farms, " April 18, 2019 at https://www.agweb.com/article/how-prenuptial-agreements-protect-farms

Cari Rincker, "Top 10 Reasons Why Prenups are Romantic for Farmers and Ranchers," at https://feedlotmagazine.com/top-10-reasons-why-prenups-are-romantic-for-farmers-and-ranchers/

CHAPTER 2

DIVORCE VS. SEPARATION

In almost every consultation that I have had, one of the questions that I inevitably ask potential clients is, "are you sure the marriage is irretrievably broken? Is reconciliation possible?" That conversation usually leads to a discussion about divorce vs. legal separation.

Put simply, folks should consider separation vs. divorce in two scenarios: (1) there is some type of legal reason to stay married or (2) there is a chance, albeit small, of reconciliation. If neither of these apply to your situation, then divorce is the proper path.

The term "legal separation" is oftentimes confused. *In order to be "legally separated" then technically speaking, there should be a separation agreement that has been filed with the court and a Judgment of Separation.* When two people are living separate and apart, there is nothing "legal" about this.

It's the written, signed (and sometimes notarized, depending on your jurisdiction) separation agreement and court order/judgment that make this separation formal. Some prefer to have that structure while other families are okay with an oral temporary separation agreement. This is an important discussion to have with your counterpart.

Importantly, folks can be "legally separated" for as long as they want – the divorce is not automatically granted after a certain period of time. In states like New York, however, either party can ask for a separation once a statutory period has elapsed – for example, New York requires one year of continuous separation without reconciliation, sexually speaking, living pursuant to a separation agreement. Subsequently, either party can ask the court for a *conversion divorce, but* that is only if either side requests this.

For those interested in going down the separation path, the first question you need to ask yourself is "why?" If the answer to that question is potential reconciliation, then it is recommended to have a game plan that may include, but is not limited to:

1. Therapy or couples counseling/family counseling;
2. Counseling through your church or religious community;
3. Use of a trained conciliator (conciliation is short for "reconciliation"); and
4. Other resources to help mend relationships and families.

Rincker Law, PLLC, can provide referrals for these types of professionals in the jurisdictions that we practice in; alternatively, I suggest reaching out to a family lawyer in your local community for these types of resources. A written separation agreement can include agreements that each party will attend counseling in good faith for X duration.

The decision on whether to get a divorce or work through the rough patch with a (legal) separation is highly personal and specific to each individual family and circumstances. *As I like to tell clients, "you cannot unring the divorce bell" so be careful on entering this path if you are unsure.* The D word should not be thrown around lightly and it is rare (but not impossible) for families to reconcile once one person files for divorce.

CHAPTER 3

OVERVIEW OF THE DIVORCE PROCESS

Not only does the divorce process change from state to state, but it can also vary somewhat from county to county within that jurisdiction. This chapter has a typical divorce procedure in Illinois, but it will give a nice overview of the general process. States like New York have a contested or uncontested track with very different paths. It is important to discuss what divorces look like in your state.

FILING A DIVORCE

Divorces require making a petition or complaint to the court like any legal action. States like Illinois call the parties "Petitioner" and "Respondent," while states like New York call the parties "Plaintiff" and "Defendant."

It does not make a legal difference on who is the Petitioner and who is the Respondent. The divorce is commenced by filing a Petition for the Dissolution of the Marriage in Illinois, whereas it is called a Summons with Notice or Summons and a Verified Complaint in New York – either way, there is some initiating pleading for the action. The filing fee for divorces differs from localities.

COMMENCEMENT AND SERVICE OF DIVORCE OF PAPERS

After filing the divorce, the other party will need to be served. If the spouse is cooperative then an acceptance of service can be filed by that party or his/her/their counsel.

For those spouses that need to be personally served, typically a process server or the police are used (depending on state). Once your spouse is served, then he/she has 20 to 30 days to "appear" in this action (timing can vary from state-to-state). This requires a spouse to appear on his or her own or via a lawyer by filing an Entry/Notice of Appearance.

NEGOTIATING THE SETTLEMENT AGREEMENT

The next stage is negotiating global settlement, if at all possible. In some cases, this cannot be done until later in the case. There is no "one size fits all" pattern with divorces as each family and their circumstances is unique.

Illinois likes to break up the settlement agreement in two: (1) the Marital Settlement Agreement ("MSA") and (2) the Parenting Plan (if applicable). Other states like New York can combine these into one master Stipulation of Settlement or Separation Agreement discussing all issues.

Regardless on the naming of the documents or how the parties and counsel break them up, they will discuss the following issues (but are not limited to):

1. Division of household effects;
2. Division of other assets and liabilities, if applicable;
3. Spousal maintenance;
4. Child support; and
5. Allocation of parental responsibilities (i.e., custody and visitation/parenting time).

Negotiation can take place in one of three ways: (1) between you and your spouse directly, (2) between the two lawyers (if applicable), or (3) using ADR, such as mediation or arbitration.

Direct negotiation between you and your spouse may or may not be productive. You know your relationship with your spouse better than your lawyer does but you should consult with your lawyer directly before doing so. For some families, they are able to calmly discuss some issues for the MSA while other issues may need to be negotiated between lawyers.

Attorney to attorney negotiation is the most common form of negotiation for a divorce. This may be done with emails, letters, telephone calls, or face-to-face meetings, depending on the style of the attorneys and the type of issues being negotiated. I have found that written correspondence can be a productive way to begin negotiation.

A "Four-Way Settlement Conference" may be used, i.e., the four parties includes both lawyers and both parties. Friends, family members, and children should not attend this meeting. If productive, it is possible that multiple "Four-Ways" may be held. In person (vs telephonic) "Four-Ways" are preferred.

CONSIDER ADR

As discussed in more detail in another chapter, there are a few different forms of ADR applicable to divorces including:

1. Mediation;
2. Arbitration; and
3. Early Neutral Evaluation

Here is a brief overview of each type:

1.   Mediation. Mediation is the most common form of ADR in a divorce. A mediator is there to facilitate a conversation between the two of you to discuss the applicable issues. A mediation session is usually between 1.5 to 2.5 hours for each session and it can sometimes take about 2 to 5 (or more) mediation sessions to reach a global settlement. The role of the mediator is not to provide you legal advice, that is the role of the attorneys.

2.   Arbitration. Arbitration is akin to a trial where the arbitrator acts like a judge reviewing documents provided by both sides and making either a binding or non-binding decision for the two of you. In Illinois, an arbitrator can only be used for economic decisions for the divorce and can never be used for determining issues of child custody and visitation.

3.   Early Neutral Evaluation. Early Neutral Evaluation is a growing but more rare form of ADR. Like an arbitrator, a neutral evaluator is an experienced professional who reviews arguments and documents from each party. The neutral evaluator gives an opinion on what he/she believes an experienced jurist would decide. This can be particularly helpful if the parties are at an impasse.

Please note that a collaborative divorce is a different model.

In this form of ADR, a mediator is used while both parties are represented by their own consulting attorney. Both parties agree in writing that, if either goes to court, they will go get new attorneys. Other professionals are sometimes used in this model such as accountants, financial advisors and therapists.

More information on this can also be found in my book "ONWARD AND UPWARD: GUIDE FOR GETTING THROUGH NEW YORK DIVORCE AND FAMILY LAW ISSUES" available on Amazon, Kindle, and iBooks. Although the book discusses New York family law, the chapters on ADR are applicable in other states.

DISCOVERY

It is common for the parties to voluntarily exchange Financial Affidavits/Statements of Net Worth and financial documents such as:

1. Tax returns;
2. Pay stubs;
3. Bank statements; and
4. Credit card statements.

For farmers, be prepared to inventory farm equipment and livestock. Appraisals may have to be done. The discovery process can be brief and informal or it can take years, depending on the complexity of the financial issues.

IF A SETTLEMENT IS REACHED

There are only two ways to a divorce – settlement or trial. If you are able to reach an agreement on the issues, the settlement agreement(s) is finalized. This can be drafted by either attorney or the mediator. Both sides may go back and forth in finalizing the details. "The devil is in the details," so to speak, so this process can take a while.

The Judgment for the Dissolution of Marriage/Judgment of Divorce, Certificate of Dissolution and any other documents that the court requires will need to be finalized. New York requires an entire "uncontested divorce packet," while other states like North Carolina require few documents.

Depending on the state, a final court date may need to be

scheduled to finalize the matter – this may be called a "prove-up" or "inquest" where there is an allocution of the agreement on the record.

In states like New York, the finalization process may take six to eight months, depending on county, so it is important to discuss this directly with your local attorney.

AFTER THE DIVORCE

After the divorce is final, the work is not over yet. There may be Qualified Domestic Relations Orders, Quit Claim Deeds, or other documents that need to be signed to deal with the transfer of assets. There might also be name change steps that need to be performed. *After a divorce, both parties should also revisit their estate plans.*

CHAPTER 4

CHILD SUPPORT

Child support in most states is largely formulaic (i.e., a math equation). Basic support is typically calculated by looking at the income and qualified deductions of each parent. However, for most involved in farming and ranching or other kind of agribusiness, finding the numbers for the math equation is anything but straightforward. This figure is also used to help calculate child add-on expenses such as:

1. Health insurance;
2. Unreimbursed medical expenses;
3. Day care/childcare expenses (which can include camp);
4. Educational expenses (e.g., school supplies, tutoring, school registration); and
5. Extracurricular expenses.

Mandatory and discretionary child expenses vary from state to state. Private school tuition is usually discretionary upon the court and is based on the income of the parties.

CALCULATING SUPPORT

The exact equation for calculating child support does vary from state to state. In some states like New York, an income cap is used. Nearly every state has "deviation factors" that allow the court to adjust basic child support either upwards or downwards based on the statutory factors (e.g., standard of living the child would have enjoyed had the household stayed intact; special needs/medical needs of the child; financial resources of the child).

Business owners, including farmers, ranchers, and food entrepreneurs, do not have straight-forward income. Accelerated depreciation, prepays, and other deductions that support living expenses can be added back to the obligor's income for purposes of this equation. Courts typically have discretion on any such adjustments. If the farm or agribusiness pays for living expenses, such as housing, mobile phone, vehicle expenses, food/entertainment, etc. then the court can also input this as income for child support purposes.

> *Example: Farmer John used accelerated depreciation for a $100K combine over 1 year. The family farm also pays for Farmer John's cellular phone bill, truck/vehicle expenses, and housing expenses. Farmer Susie can argue that said monies be added back to John's IRS income of $25K when calculating child support – this is discretionary upon the court and varies from state to state.*

EMANCIPATION

The age of emancipation for child support purposes varies from state to state. Some states, like New York, choose an age of emancipation of 21 years, while most states choose the age of 18 or graduation from high school, whichever is later (but no more than age 19). Additionally, the child will also be considered emancipated upon marriage or entry into the military. This is a negotiated point with farm divorces as the parents may voluntarily agree to extend child support obligation through the age of 22 or through an undergraduate degree (or even graduate school, if applicable). Oftentimes, courts will allow parties to seek post-majority support if the child is attending college. Parents can also seek court intervention to extend the date of emancipation if the child has special needs and is dependent on the parents.

POST-SECONDARY EXPENSES OR POST-MAJORITY SUPPORT

College expenses are a hot topic in divorces. Sometimes divorcing couples choose to wait until the children are at the age of 16 or 17 and college feels more imminent, while others want to address the issue at the time of the divorce. Courts will often cap required contributions to college to a cap based on tuition for the state university; however, parents can agree on a lower or higher cap depending on the circumstances and income of the parties.

LIFE INSURANCE

Life insurance can be used as payment security for child support payments (including college expenses) in the event of death. This is usually a negotiated point; it can be ordered by the court, but it is typically voluntary. Term life insurance is used in these instances and the required amount can decrease each year and as the total child support obligation decreases. This may also be done for spousal support, if applicable.

MODIFICATION

Importantly, child support can be revisited. Most states allow for child support to be modified when there has been a substantial change in circumstances (e.g., significant change in income). Some states specify that either party may revisit support after a certain number of years. Divorcing parents may choose to exchange tax returns every year to help ascertain if child support should be adjusted; some refer to this annual check-up as a "true up" and require the same in their divorce settlement agreement.

CONCLUSION

As one can imagine, this can become a problematic math equation because it requires a thorough review of tax returns and other business financials. Farmers, ranchers, and agribusiness owners are advised to consult an experienced family law attorney with a food and agriculture background to help negotiate a fair agreement for child support.

CHAPTER 5

CHILD CUSTODY AND VISITATION

Divorcing farm and ranch families with children invariably have to consider custody and visitation issues. This chapter first discuss custody and then visitation.

Importantly, the law varies from state to state on which factors the court considers when determining what is in the best interests of the children. Divorcing farm families should consult a lawyer in his or her jurisdiction to understand the list of statutory or factors established by case law. Such factors typically include the (a) wishes of the child (depending on age); (b) wishes of the parents; (c) historic caretaking and decision-making; (d) ability for a parent to facilitate a relationship with the other parent; (e) any history of abuse; (f) distance between the parents; (g) relationship between the parents, etc.

CUSTODY

Importantly, there is a growing trend for states to move away from the term "custody" because the term sparks so much emotion. *States such as Illinois have moved to calling it "allocation of parental responsibilities."* Regardless of the terminology, there are two types of custody: (1) residence and (2) decision-making.

As for the primary residence of the children, if the children live with one parent 51% or more of the time, then that parent has primary residence (sometimes referred to as sole physical custody or primary residential custody). If the parents have a pure 50/50 arrangement, then there is no primary residence, and the parents have joint physical custody.

With decision-making, this refers to major decisions, not day-to-day decisions such as brushing hair, doing homework, bedtime routine, etc. In most states, the applicable major decision applies to four spheres of influence: (1) non-emergency health; (2) religion; (3) education; and (4) extracurricular activities. There are several choices with decision making and it is not related to physical custody. In other words, the parents can have joint legal custody even though only one parent has the primary residence with the children.

If the parents agree on joint decision making, then there are several options:

1. Pure joint decision-making;
2. After good-faith consultation, then the custodial parent has the final say or tie-breaking vote;
3. After good-faith consultation, the parents divide who has the tie-breaking vote 50/50 (e.g., the mother have final decision making on health or religion while the father has final decision-making on education and extracurricular);
4. After good faith consultation, if the parents are still at an impasse, then they agree to go to mediation (or possibly add a tie-break step if mediation is futile); and
5. After good faith consultation, then a third-party decides (e.g., a parent coordinator, general doctor for health decisions, school counselor for educational decisions, pastor for religious decisions).

Which option is chosen depends on the relationship between the parties and what is in the best interests of the children.

PARENTING TIME

Some parents prefer to have a loose schedule, which is referred to as liberal parenting time; however, most families prefer a dependable schedule. Parenting time is best to be broken up into (a) basic schedule; (b) school break schedule; (c) summer break schedule; and (d) holiday parenting time.

BASIC SCHEDULE

This is when school is in session and while there are no major holidays or school breaks. It is the "default schedule." It is suggested that parents think about this schedule over a few-week time period.

Here is an example blank worksheet:

Week	M	T	W	R	F	S	S
W1							
W2							
W3							
W4							

There are unlimited combinations with the basic schedule. Parents should "reality test" potential schedules by thinking about the age of the children, distance between the parents, school logistics, extracurricular activities (such as 4-H, including 4-H animals, and sports), church, etc.

For those parents considering joint parenting time, here are some options for 50/50 plans:

2/2/3 (Rotation)

Week	M	T	W	R	F	S	S
W1	Dad	Dad	Mom	Mom	Dad	Dad	Dad
W2	Mom	Mom	Dad	Dad	Mom	Mom	Mom
W3	Dad	Dad	Mom	Mom	Dad	Dad	Dad
W4	Mom	Mom	Dad	Dad	Mom	Mom	Mom

2/2/3 Schedule (Same Parent with M-T/W-R)

Week	M	T	W	R	F	S	S
W1	Dad[1]	Dad	Mom	Mom	Dad	Dad	Dad
W2	Dad	Dad	Mom	Mom	Mom	Mom	Mom
W3	Dad	Dad	Mom	Mom	Dad	Dad	Dad
W4	Dad	Dad	Mom	Mom	Mom	Mom	Mom

2/3/2 Schedule – Alternating Wednesdays and Weekends (Same Parent M-T/R-F)

Week	M	T	W	R	F	S	S
W1	Mom	Mom	Dad	Dad	Dad	Mom	Mom
W2	Mom	Mom	Mom	Dad	Dad	Dad	Dad
W3	Mom	Mom	Dad	Dad	Dad	Mom	Mom
W4	Mom	Mom	Mom	Dad	Dad	Dad	Dad

---

[1] Mom and Dad are used here for illustrative purposes only. The family may have two Moms or two Dads.

3/4 Schedule (Same Parent M-T-W/F-S-S with Alternating Thursdays)

Week	M	T	W	R	F	S	S
W1	Mom	Mom	Mom	Dad	Dad	Dad	Dad
W2	Mom	Mom	Mom	Mom	Dad	Dad	Dad
W3	Mom	Mom	Mom	Dad	Dad	Dad	Dad
W4	Mom	Mom	Mom	Mom	Dad	Dad	Dad

3/4 Schedule (7 days in a row/split weeks)

Week	M	T	W	R	F	S	S
W1	Mom	Mom	Mom	Dad	Dad	Dad	Dad
W2	Dad	Dad	Dad	Mom	Mom	Mom	Mom
W3	Mom	Mom	Mom	Dad	Dad	Dad	Dad
W4	Dad	Dad	Dad	Mom	Mom	Mom	Mom

Alternating Weekends Plus 2 Midweek Schedule

Week	M	T	W	R	F	S	S
W1	Mom	Dad	Dad	Mom	Dad	Dad	Dad
W2	Mom	Dad	Dad	Mom	Mom	Mom	Mom
W3	Mom	Dad	Dad	Mom	Dad	Dad	Dad
W4	Mom	Dad	Dad	Mom	Mom	Mom	Mom

4/4 Schedule

Week	M	T	W	R	F	S	S
W1	Dad	Dad	Dad	Dad	Mom	Mom	Mom
W2	Mom	Dad	Dad	Dad	Dad	Mom	Mom
W3	Mom	Mom	Dad	Dad	Dad	Dad	Mom
W4	Mom	Mom	Mom	Dad	Dad	Dad	Dad

7/7 Schedule

Week	M	T	W	R	F	S	S
W1	Dad	Dad	Dad	Dad	Dad	Dad	Dad
W2	Mom	Mom	Mom	Mom	Mom	Mom	Mom
W3	Dad	Dad	Dad	Dad	Dad	Dad	Dad
W4	Mom	Mom	Mom	Mom	Mom	Mom	Mom

SCHOOL BREAK SCHEDULE

Schools vary on their school breaks. Typically, there is a four-day weekend for Thanksgiving Break, a few weeks for Christmas/Winter Break, and Spring Break (which is normally a week long). Schools in some geographic regions, like New York, add a fourth school break in February on President's Day week (called the Mid-Winter Break). Schools that are year-long have their own unique calendar. Parents need to evaluate this in accordance with their children's calendar.

Here is an example worksheet with school breaks:

School Break	Description	Odd-Numbered Years	Even-Numbered Years
Thanksgiving	4-day weekend		
Winter/Christmas			
Mid-Winter Recess (President's Day) (some schools)			
Spring Break			

SUMMER BREAK SCHEDULE

Farm and ranch families involved in 4-H, FFA, livestock breed organizations, or other agriculture organizations require special attention for the summer schedule. Some parents decide to have a certain number of consecutive or nonconsecutive weeks' vacation in the summer while other parents may agree on alternating weeks or on following the basic school schedule. Agriculture parents should consider the summer routine of the children, especially if it applies to 4-H and other agriculture activities.

HOLIDAY PARENTING TIME

Finally, parents should think through holiday parenting time. Again, this schedule will supersede all the other schedules. The first step is for parents to think about what holidays they have observed historically. Typically, parents will alternate those holidays every other year, but some holidays may always be assigned to one parent (e.g., Mother's Day, Father's Day).

Here is an example worksheet on holidays:

TRADITIONAL HOLIDAYS

Holiday	Odd Years	Even Years
New Year's Eve		
New Year's Day		
Martin Luther King Jr. Day		
Easter		
Mother's Day		
Memorial Day		
Father's Day		
Independence Day		
Labor Day		
Columbus Day		
Halloween		
Veteran's Day		
Thanksgiving		
Christmas Eve		
Christmas		

ADDITIONAL HOLIDAYS (INCLUDING RELIGIOUS HOLIDAYS, BIRTHDAYS)

Holiday	Odd Years	Even Years
Child's Birthday		

CONCLUSION

This chapter just hits the tip of the iceberg on custody and visitation issues. Ancillary issues include, but are not limited to: information sharing; relocation provisions; telephone/video conference access; travel (including itinerary requirements); co-parenting applications (e.g., Our Family Wizard, Talking Parents); or using a shared calendar like Google Calendar, and ADR (such as mediation). Grandparent or sibling visitation (if half-siblings) may also be discussed.

CHAPTER 6

USE OF THIRD PARTIES IN CUSTODY

DISPUTES

Depending on your jurisdiction, there may be third parties who will be involved in custody and visitation disputes such as Guardians ad Litem, attorneys for the child, custody evaluators, or therapists who do psychological evaluations. There are few specific nuances with the use of these professionals that apply to farm families; however, it is important that whoever is involved with your divorce and separation that these persons better understanding the dynamics of your farm and ranch family.

GUARDIANS AD LITEM

Some states like Illinois use Guardians ad Litem (or if you're in Champaign County, Limited Guardians ad Litem). Guardians ad Litem ("GAL") are effectively the "eyes and ears of the court" and are oftentimes lawyers, but are not the attorneys for either party or the child.

The GAL conducts a thorough investigation. The GAL should make the child's preference known to the court and the court is required to give some weight to the GAL's recommendation. It is discretionary upon the court to appoint a GAL and is reserved for contested child custody cases with more significant disputes between the parents on the primary residence and the allocation of parental responsibilities.

The GAL acts under the control and discretion of the court, acting as both a pro se party on the child's behalf and an independent expert witness. There is no power to have privileged and confidential conversations with the child. Importantly, the GAL is not your lawyer and anything said to the GAL by you or the child may be said in court.

The GAL attends pre-trial court appearances, trial, and post-decree proceedings. The GAL can file pleadings, conduct depositions, testify, call witnesses, present a closing argument, and file post-decree motions, if necessary, like any pro se party.

The GAL may wish to interview additional persons about a case such as other family members, teachers, counselors, or the parents' attorneys. The GAL may also request copies of records such as medical records, counseling, and school records.

The GAL will be writing a final report to the court. There may be interim reports to advise the court of any matters at the pre-trial conference. The parents' attorneys will have access to the report. Although the parents would have the opportunity to review the report with their attorneys, the court may not allow the parents to have a copy of the report. During the hearing, the parents' attorneys will be able to question the GAL regarding the report and any opinions/recommendations that the GAL makes to the court.

In his or her dual role as an independent expert witness, the GAL has broad powers of investigation and makes recommendations to the court pursuant to rules of civil procedure. The GAL may testify as to his or her personal observations and offer an in-court expert opinion concerning the best interests of the child based on his or her investigation. Importantly, this "expert opinion" is limited to his or her level of expertise. To illustrate, the GAL cannot testify as to a parent's psychological state of mind or disorder. However, the GAL may:

1. Ask questions of the witnesses (including the parents);
2. Testify as to his or her report; and
3. Call his or her own witnesses to protect the subject child(ren).

As far as fees are concerned, the GAL will be billing for his or her time. The GAL's billing will be presented to the court on a regular basis. Additional fees may be required if litigation continues in the case.

ATTORNEYS FOR THE CHILD

States like New York have attorneys for the child instead of Guardians ad Litem. Even states that have Guardians ad Litem, such as Illinois, may also choose to use an attorney for the child in special circumstances.

An attorney for the child is just that – an attorney who represents the child. Parents sometimes are mistaken that this attorney is a neutral third party or an attorney for themselves. This is not the case. There is no attorney-client privilege between the parents and the attorney for the child; conversely, there is attorney client privilege between the child(ren) and the attorney for the child.

This attorney for the child is in an advocacy role and can draft motions and will attend court likely the other attorneys. This person can ask questions on cross-examination and call witnesses likely any other attorney. Depending on the age and maturity of the child, the attorney for the child will take the position of the child in court, even if this position is unreasonable.

CUSTODY EVALUATIONS

Depending on the law in your state, there may be custody evaluations ordered (or some variation thereof). This section is based on custody evaluations in Illinois. As always, consult with a lawyer in your jurisdiction for more information specific to your situation.

STEP 1: CONTACT THE EVALUATOR TO MAKE APPOINTMENTS

It is important to contact the evaluator as soon as possible. You may want to also share the contact information of any witnesses, collateral contacts, etc., including any persons living in your home.

STEP 2: PAYMENT TERMS

Your fees may be on a flat fee or hourly basis. Be sure to understand the fee structure. The court and the evaluator may take a negative inference if payment is delayed. Please note that this fee may increase if it requires an unusual amount of work or travel. Interviews with the custody evaluator after the report will likely surpass this flat fee; additionally, the expert will have added fees if he/she is asked to testify.

STEP 3: SEND MATERIALS AND CONTACTS TO THE CUSTODY EVALUATOR

The next step is to gather up relevant documentation for the review by the evaluator with the supervision and advice of counsel, such as relevant pleadings, court transcripts, proposed parenting plans, medical records, police reports, photographs, school records, text messages/email correspondence with the other parent, etc. Please do not send this documentation directly to the custody evaluator as your attorney's office will organize and produce same to the evaluator, copying opposing counsel.

Furthermore, like a Guardian ad Litem evaluation, your attorney may wish to send 3 to 5 contacts that the evaluator may choose to interview. Depending on the evaluator, he or she may not choose to interview these contacts, but may choose to do so. The child's therapist or school counselor may be good choices as contacts. If there has been a DCFS investigation, then the contact information for the caseworker should be included. A parent should also discuss gathering support letters from family and friends with his or her attorney.

STEP 4: PSYCHOLOGICAL TESTING

Parents should be prepared for psychological testing to take the entire day. Depending on the evaluator, you could be at the office for 5 to 8 hours (i.e., 6 hours is typical).

The evaluation begins the moment you step through the door. Your interactions with reception and staff will be noted. Parents should be as cooperative and respectful to staff as possible, including in the signing of paperwork.

The evaluator will take notes on how you are dressed that day. You do not need to wear a suit, but you should be dressed nicely. Because you will be in testing for most of the day, you should dress comfortably. Do not wear jeans and a sweatshirt. Open toed shoes should be avoided. The evaluator will likely make notes on your physical appearance so be sure to put your best foot forward from a standpoint of your presentation.

It is possible that one person will be asked to take the tests in the same office as the evaluator while the other is in a conference room. Please take note of this for your attorney's reference only but do not make comments about impartiality to the evaluator.

Depending on the case, the evaluator will offer a series of psychological tests. Understandably, this can be overwhelming, but just take it one question at a time and try to answer truthfully and honestly. The testing is developed to look for deceptive behavior. Be prepared that your answers for the custody and parenting questionnaire may be added into the report directly. The report may quote you exactly; thus, think carefully about your verbiage and do not disparage the other parent, the lawyers, or the judge.

STEP 5: HOME STUDY

During this portion of the visit, the evaluator will visit both parents' homes and visit the child in his or her natural environment during parenting time. The evaluator will also want to interview any other persons living in the home, such as partners, other children, or family members. Be sure to make these persons available.

The custody evaluator will look at the house, interview the child, and ask you questions about the living environment. Please make sure the house is clean and tidy for this visit. The parent should budget for this to last anywhere from 1.5 to 2.5 hours (i.e., two hour average). It is also a good idea to put cell phones on silent during this period.

STEP 6: CLINICAL INTERVIEW

This is the last stage of the forensic psychological evaluation. This interview will likely be at the custody evaluator's office and is usually after both the psychological testing and home study.

PSYCHOLOGICAL EVALUATIONS

It is unlikely that you will have psychological evaluations, in addition to a custody evaluations, as a psychological evaluation is likely a component of a custody evaluation; however, this can be ordered in any battle with the allocation of parental responsibilities (or custody) if the court has concerns about the psychological fitness of one or both parents.

CHAPTER 7

SPOUSAL SUPPORT

Spousal maintenance in some states is formulaic, while others rely on case law. In either scenario, there needs to be a determination of income (not assets). For most involved in farming and ranching or other kinds of agribusiness, determining income is anything but straightforward. Typically, a spouse is required to pay for his/her health insurance after the divorce, but if he/she has serious medical issues, then this can be a negotiated add-on.

THE FORMULA

The equation for calculating spousal support does vary from state to state. In some states, like New York, an income cap is used. Nearly every state has "deviation factors" that allow the court to adjust spousal maintenance either upwards or downwards based on the statutory factors (e.g., standard of living during the marriage, medical issues). Some states do not have a formula, but looks at the circumstances in that case.

Business owners, including farmers, ranchers, and food entrepreneurs, do not have straight-forward income. Accelerated depreciation, prepays, and other deductions can be added back to the payor's income for the purposes of this equation. Courts typically have discretion on these adjustments. If the farm or agribusiness pays for living expenses, such as housing, mobile phone, vehicle expenses, and food/entertainment, then the court can also input this as income for spousal support purposes.

As one can imagine, this can become a problematic calculation for business owners because it requires a thorough review of tax returns and other business financials. Farmers, ranchers, and agribusiness owners are advised to consult a family law attorney with food and agriculture background to help negotiate a fair agreement for spousal support to fit the specific circumstances.

DURATION

Duration of spousal maintenance is also a negotiated point. Some states, like Illinois, have memorialized durations based on the number of years of marriage up to 20 years. At this point, the payee should receive maintenance for the length of the marriage or for an indefinite term. Other states, like New York, have set forth ranges, giving the court discretion (e.g., if the marriage is less than 15 years, then maintenance will be between 15% to 30%, depending on the length of the marriage). Other states rely on case law and give the trial judge wide discretion. Importantly, permanent maintenance (i.e., alimony) is uncommon in most states with limited exceptions. Most states prefer durational maintenance (i.e., maintenance for a duration).

Spousal maintenance typically terminates in the following instances:

1. Upon the death of the payor;
2. Upon the death of the payee;
3. Upon the end of the specified duration (e.g., 5 years, 10 years);
4. Remarriage of the payee; or
5. Cohabitation of the payee.

Cohabitation is more than just having a significant other. It is living with one another in a conjugal relationship and sharing expenses, much like a married couple would. There is a myriad of other factors the court considers and, again, this can vary from state to state.

USING LIFE INSURANCE TO SECURE MAINTENANCE

Life insurance can be used as payment security for spousal support payments in the event of death. This is oftentimes a negotiated point; it can be ordered by the court, but it is usually voluntary. Term life insurance is used in these instances and the required amount can decrease each year and as the necessary maintenance decreases. This may also be done for child support, if applicable.

By Cari B. Rincker, Esq.

CHAPTER 8

EQUITABLE DISTRIBUTION

Equitable distribution ("ED") is the allocation of the marital estate in a divorce. Importantly, not all states are equitable distribution states; instead, states like Texas and California are community property states. The majority of states are equitable distribution states, but it is important to confirm this with a licensed attorney in the applicable jurisdiction.

In way of background, property in a marriage fits into one of three buckets: two separate (or nonmarital) property buckets and the marital property bucket.

Spouse 1 Bucket	Marital Bucket	Spouse 2 Bucket

Prenuptial or postnuptial agreements can help identify what are in the various buckets. Absent a nuptial agreement, the definition of what fits in each bucket can vary from state-to-state and can change overtime.

The concept of "equitable distribution" means "fair and just" distribution, not "equal distribution." It is a common misconception that people in a divorce split property 50/50. How marital property is divided can be set forth in the nuptial agreement, if applicable (e.g., 50/50, pro rata based on income, or some type of agreed-upon equation or division). If there is no contractual agreement on how to divide the marital state, then equitable distribution states set forth factors that the court is to consider when determining the fair division of assets. Trial courts have broad discretion on making this determination. Some judges have certain tendencies with equitable distribution (i.e., some are more attracted to 50/50 splits than others).

This chapter discusses a simple 4 step analysis: (1) identification of separate property; (2) identification of marital property; (3) valuation of property; and (4) equitable distribution of marital assets.

IDENTIFICATION OF SEPARATE (OR NONMARITAL) AND MARITAL PROPERTY

The first step in the analysis is to divide property in the three buckets. Again, the law can vary somewhat from state to state on what property fits into each bucket, and there can even be sophisticated nuances in some areas in the same jurisdiction. Here are a few examples of property that is in the separate property bucket:

1. Gifts (except for joint gifts or wedding gifts);
2. Inheritance (except if in joint name);
3. Premarital property; and
4. Property from a personal injury award (excluding lost wages).

Keep in mind that the definition of property is broad. It can include intellectual property (e.g., trademarks), business interests, retirement/pensions, animals, farm equipment, etc. The most overlooked property in a farm or ranch divorce is the business itself.

As a caveat, separate property can transfer to the marital property bucket if funds are commingled or they are in joint name. This is called transmutation. For example, if a premarital piece of farm equipment was sold and deposited into the joint bank account, then those monies are now part of the marital bucket. That said, some states allow for "separate property credits."

> *If Farmer John had premarital farmland that was sold during the marriage and $50K of the proceeds were used as a down payment on a marital residence in joint name, then Farmer John may have a claim to get his $50K down payment back on a dollar-for-dollar basis.*

Income and appreciation of separate property muddy the

waters. States vary significantly in this area and some jurisdictions look into whether the non-titled spouse had either active or passive involvement in the appreciation or whether the appreciation was strictly due to market forces.

Importantly, the person claiming separate property has the burden of proof.

> *Example: Farmer Jane had a $200K retirement account at the time of the marriage and it increased to $500K during the marriage, then Farmer Jane would need to prove that the value at the date of the marriage was $200K. It is difficult to obtain documentation more than seven years of age by subpoena to financial institutions, so hopefully Farmer Jane kept good records and can find this statement. If she cannot, then Farmer Jane can hire an actuary to do a sophisticated analysis with the known statements. The point is this: if Farmer Jane wants to keep the $200K premarital property (plus any appreciation thereof, depending on her state), then she has to do the work to find the proof.*

A word on debt – it too fits into these same three buckets. If one person comes to the marriage with student loan debt or a mortgage on premarital property, then it is considered separate debt. When people walk down the aisle, their debt liability does not get "cut in half" as some people may assume. Although states differ in this regard, as a general rule, spouses are jointly and severally liable for debt during the marriage only. It is not unusual for people to think they are no longer responsible for the debt of their spouse once they "separate." Unfortunately for some, that is not always the case. Of course, they may have wasteful dissipation claims or equitable arguments once divorce papers are filed, but parties should keep this in mind during the divorce.

IDENTIFICATION OF MARITAL PROPERTY

The work in this analysis is pulling out the separate property. Everything that does not fit into a separate property bucket is considered party of the marital bucket. These lists should be detailed and may include grain inventory, farm equipment inventory, and livestock. Marital debt and prepaid expenses should also be on this list.

VALUATION OF PROPERTY

Property should then be valued, if appropriate. This is where appraisers can be used to appraise real property, farm equipment, art, or other valuable items. It may be difficult to find a livestock appraiser, but auctioneers may feel comfortable in doing so.

Do not forget to value the business. Business evaluators should be used to value the farm/ranch/agribusiness itself; in doing so, typically 5+ years of tax returns, bank statements, and other financial records are reviewed. If a farming enterprise has several entities, then each needs to be valued separately (e.g., sole proprietorship, family partnership, trucking company, restaurant).

Crops in the ground are difficult to value, but are absolutely considered an asset for a farm divorce.

EQUITABLE DISTRIBUTION OF MARITAL PROPERTY

The last and final step in the analysis is to decide how to divide the marital bucket fairly and equitably. There is a myriad of factors that are considered with this determination, often enumerated in the state statute. Some factors such as the "length of the marriage" may be weighed more heavily than other factors such as contribution to the marital estate, tax consequences, spousal support, etc. Courts look at the totality of the circumstances in deciding what is fair.

The longer the marriage, the more courts will lean towards a 50/50 split in equity. Even with long marriages, courts may decide to deviate and give one spouse more or less depending on the facts and circumstances. For example, the court may credit one spouse if the other spouse wastefully dissipated marital assets by gambling, drug or alcohol abuse, frivolous purchases, etc. Courts may also give more than 50% of the estate to a spouse with significantly less earning power than the other spouse.

Keep in mind that families do not have to liquidate assets in order to divide property. One spouse may keep the farmland, farm equipment, and cows, while the other gets the retirement, investment property, and farm vehicles, depending on the arithmetic. Spouses can "buy" each other out or negotiate long-term payment plans for farm business interests.

Furthermore, spouses can also decide not to break up the farm and keep it intact; in this scenario, the divorcing spouses remain business partners. Language should be carefully crafted on paying distributions to the owners, responsibilities of each owner, and buy-out provisions in case one or both ex-spouses decide to go their separate way in business.

There are no hard and fast rules with equitable distribution. Unfortunately, there are the shades of grey with equitable distribution that make divorce litigation expensive. After all, no two families are the same and neither are their asset distributions. To keep costs down, parties are encouraged to cooperate with discovery and consider Alternative Dispute Resolution, such as mediation or arbitration for economic issues.

CHAPTER 9

COMMUNITY PROPERTY

A handful of states, including *Texas, California, Arizona, Washington, Idaho, Nevada, New Mexico and Wisconsin* are considered "Community Property" states with the remainder being equitable distribution states. Alaska has an "opt-in" law as it applies to community property. In some ways, Connecticut is a quasi-community property state. It is important to confirm this with a licensed attorney in the applicable jurisdiction as there are differences from state-to-state as there are no cut and dry rules.

In Community Property ("CP") states, property fits into one of two categories: separate property or community property. All property acquired during the marriage is presumed community property and remaining property is characterized as separate property. Separate property is any property owned prior to the marriage, inherited property, and property that is gifted to one spouse. A spouse seeking to prove certain property is separate property has the burden to prove so through clear and convincing evidence.

Property that is characterized as CP must be divided upon divorce. While CP may often be split equally between spouses, it is a common misconception that people in a divorce always split property 50/50. The court may deviate from this standard using various factors to ensure the division is "just and right" which may not necessarily be an equal division. How community property is divided can be set forth in the nuptial agreement, if applicable (e.g., 50/50, pro rata based on income, or some type of agreed-upon equation or division). If there is no contractual agreement on how to divide CP, then courts divide CP. Trial courts typically divide CP equally between spouses, unless a spouse proves that this equal division is not "just and right."

This chapter discusses five items that should be considered to determine what property is CP and how it should be divided upon divorce:

1. Identification of separate and community property;
2. Income from separate property;
3. Valuation of property;
4. Prenuptial and postnuptial agreements; and
5. Division of community property and debt.

STEP 1: IDENTIFICATION OF SEPARATE AND COMMUNITY PROPERTY

Property acquired during the marriage is presumed to be CP unless the spouse claiming that it is separate property can prove otherwise through clear and convincing evidence. Therefore, the first step in the analysis is to determine what property may be characterized as separate property and then all remaining property will be considered CP. Again, the law can vary somewhat from state to state on what property fits into each category and there can even be sophisticated nuances in some areas in the same jurisdiction. A detailed property list should be drafted that includes grain inventory, farm equipment inventory, and livestock inventory. Debt acquired during marriage and prepaid expenses should also be on this list. Once a detailed list is generated, separate property may be identified.

Here are a few examples of property that is characterized as separate property:

1. Gifts (except for joint gifts or wedding gifts);
2. Inheritance (except if in joint name);
3. Premarital property; and
4. Property from a personal injury award (excluding lost wages).

Keep in mind that the definition of property is broad. It can include intellectual property (e.g., trademarks), business interests, retirement/pensions, animals, farm equipment, etc. The most overlooked property in a farm or ranch divorce is the business itself, and it is oftentimes forgotten as an asset that is either separate or community.

45

As a caveat, separate property can transfer to community property if funds are commingled or it is titled jointly in both spouses' names. This is called transmutation. For example, if a premarital piece of farm equipment was sold and deposited into the joint bank account, then those monies are now part of the CP. Livestock can also become community property absent detailed records identifying those that are separate property.

If Rancher John owned a herd of beef cattle prior to marriage that were commingled with cows purchased after marriage, the court may characterize all of his cattle as CP unless Rancher John produces clear and convincing evidence identifying which cows were owned prior to marriage.

Importantly, the burden of proof is on the person claiming separate property to show that property should be characterized as such. This person may use a method known as "tracing" and through "tracing" the spouse must determine the value of the property prior to marriage, any changes in value or character to property overtime including the sale of said property, use of proceeds from a sale of separate property to purchase community property, and changes in value of the separate property.

> *Example: If Farmer Jane had a $200K retirement account at the time of the marriage and it increased to $500K during the marriage, Farmer Jane would need to prove that the value at the date of the marriage was $200K. It is difficult to obtain documentation more than seven years of age by subpoena to financial institutions, so hopefully Farmer Jane kept good records and can find this statement. If she cannot, then Farmer Jane can hire an actuary to do a sophisticated analysis with the known statements. The point is this: if Farmer Jane wants to keep the $200K separate property (plus any appreciation thereof, depending on her state), then she has to do the work to find the proof.*

Debt must also be characterized as either separate or community. If one person comes to the marriage with student loan debt or a mortgage on separate farm ground, then it is considered separate debt. When people walk down the aisle, their debt liability does not get "cut in half" as some people may joke about at the bachelor(ette) party. Although states differ in this regard, as a general rule, spouses are jointly and severally liable for debt during the marriage only. It is not unusual for people to think they are no longer responsible for the debt of their spouse once they "separate;" unfortunately for some, that is not the case. Of course, they may have wasteful dissipation claims or equitable arguments once divorce papers are filed, but parties should keep this in mind during the divorce.

STEP 2: INCOME FROM SEPARATE PROPERTY

Income generated from and the appreciation of separate property is typically considered CP, however states vary in this area. This is particularly important for agricultural assets such as land and livestock. For example, if a spouse inherited a farm during the marriage, it is separate property, but the rents generated from that farm during the marriage are CP. Similarly, even if a spouse owned cattle prior to marriage all offspring born during the marriage are considered CP.

> *Example: Farmer Jill owns 20 dairy cows prior to marriage. During the marriage, Farmer Jill's cows raised 15 calves which were retained in the herd. The 15 calves born during the marriage are considered income and will be categorized as CP.*

STEP 3: VALUATION OF PROPERTY

Property should then be valued, if appropriate. This is where appraisers can be used to appraise real property, farm equipment, art, or other valuable items. It may be difficult to find a livestock appraiser, but auctioneers may feel comfortable in doing so.

Do not forget the value the business interest(s). Business evaluators should be used to value the farm/ranch/agribusiness itself; in doing so, typically 5+ years of tax returns, bank statements, and other financial records are reviewed. If a farming enterprise has several entities, then each needs to be valued separately (e.g., sole proprietorship, family partnership, trucking company, restaurant).

STEP 4: PRENUPTIAL OR POSTNUPTIAL AGREEMENTS

Prenuptial or postnuptial agreements can help identify the characterization of property. Absent a nuptial agreement, the definition of what fits in each category are different from state-to-state and can change over time. Specific rules to execute a valid nuptial agreement vary by state but most require that the document must include some or all of the following: (1) be in writing; (2) voluntarily signed by both parties; (3) both parties disclose all assets and liabilities; and (4) both parties waive right to any further disclosures. Each party should hire their own individual attorney to represent their interests and ensure all requirements are met according to their state's law.

A prenuptial agreement is executed prior to marriage and allows couples to identify and inventory all of their separate property. It also allows spouses to agree that income from separate property will also be separate property.

> *Example: Rancher Joe owns 30 registered breeding ewes prior to marriage. Rancher Joe and his future wife draft a prenuptial agreement. The prenuptial agreement clearly identifies Rancher Joe's 30 ewes using registration numbers and ear tattoos. It also characterizes these ewes and all future lambs born after the marriage as separate property.*

A postnuptial agreement is similar to a prenuptial agreement except that it is executed after the marriage has commenced. Unlike a prenuptial agreement, a postnuptial agreement allows spouses to characterize separate property as community property. This may be advantageous if the spouses wish for each other to inherit their separate property rather than other family members under state intestacy laws.

STEP 5: DISTRIBUTION OF COMMUNITY PROPERTY AND DEBT

The last and final step in the analysis is to decide how to divide community property and community debt. Note community property and community debt are generally split equally between the parties, but the court may deviate from equal shares if an equal split is not what is "just and right" under the circumstances.

There are a myriad of factors that are considered with this determination, oftentimes enumerated in the CP statute. Some factors include: the differences in each spouses earning potential, the needs of each spouse and children, or if a spouse was at fault (adultery, cruelty, etc.) for the divorce.

Keep in mind that families do not have to liquidate assets in order to divide property. One spouse may keep the farmland, farm equipment, and cows, while the other gets the retirement, investment property, and farm vehicles, depending on the arithmetic. Spouses can "buy" each other out or negotiate long-term payment plans for farm business interests.

Furthermore, spouses can also decide not to break up the farm and keep it intact; in this scenario, the divorcing spouses remain business partners. Language should be carefully crafted on paying distributions to the owners, responsibilities of each owner, and buy-out provisions in case one or both ex-spouses decide to go their separate way in business.

While CP is typically split equally between spouses in a divorce, litigation can become expensive if parties choose to attempt to deviate from this 50/50 split. To keep costs down, parties are encouraged to cooperate with discovery and consider ADR such as mediation or arbitration (economic issues only).

CHAPTER 10

ANIMAL LAW

Divorces among farm families often have animal issues – not only with live animals but also with genetic material (e.g., oocytes, embryos, semen). These are important property disputes for some farm families. Depending on the state, companion animals can be treated differently. It is important for divorcing farm families to think through issues with animals.

COMPANION ANIMALS

To begin, companion animals typically include dogs and cats, but can also include some exotic animals and horses. States typically take a property view when it comes to companion animals, but some jurisdictions note differences. Courts do not typically view 4-H/FFA projects as companion animals, but it is important to understand that children will have a deeper emotional connection to these animals.

Some states allow for pet visitation, while others do not. Importantly, parties are welcome to have their own negotiated or mediated agreement with pet visitation, but it is important for them to understand that depending on the state, said agreement may or may not be enforced. For example, a divorcing couple in New York will follow the "best of all concerned" standard, but will award the pet to either spouse, not allowing for pet visitation. Conversely, states like Illinois will order the "allocation of pet responsibility" and may order shared veterinary expenses and a visitation schedule.

Companion animals and pet visitation schedules may impact parenting plans in a divorce. For example, children may travel from house to house with the family dog or other companion animals. In such cases, it is prudent for families to share in veterinary expenses for the shared family pet.

Farm and ranching parties negotiating companion animal issues may consider any utility that the animal may have. For example, perhaps the dog is a sheep or cow herder or plays other roles on the farm. Horses are a special class of animals – depending on the state, they are sometimes viewed as companion animals and other states view them as livestock.

LIVESTOCK AND HORSES

Courts treat livestock and horses like any other type of property. The first step in the analysis is to ascertain if any of the animals are separate or nonmarital property. When doing so, take a look at the progeny of any gifts, inheritances, or premarital animals. Was any property commingled? Were marital assets used to pay the feed bill?

Livestock and horses should be inventoried. Make a list, including the following information:

1. Registered name (if applicable)/identified name;
2. Sex;
3. Registration number (if applicable);
4. Breed composition;
5. Color/markings (e.g., baldy);
6. Identification number (e.g., ear tag, brand, or electronic tag);
7. Tattoo number (if applicable);
8. Ear notches (if applicable);
9. Name titled in (or registered in); and
10. Location.

Depending on the jurisdiction, marital and nonmarital property needs to be valued. Appraisers or sale consultants can be hired to help value the livestock and horses to help ascertain the value of the marital estate. Animals should be appraised individually, especially with higher valued animals such as horses or a donor cow. Market animals should be valued by market prices.

FROZEN GENETICS

Eggs/oocytes, embryos, and semen should also be inventoried and valued/appraised. Parties going through a divorce will not need to hire an appraiser if they can agree upon values based on industry standards; however, if the divorcing spouses cannot agree upon the valuation of frozen genetics, then an expert should be retained. In some cases, livestock auctioneers will value the inventory list for the divorcing couple.

FINAL THOUGHTS

On a final note, it is important for couples going through a divorce to first inventory all of their assets, including farm animals and frozen genetics, and then consider if they are marital or nonmarital property. Properties should be cognizant of the inherent emotional issues affecting animals, especially companion animals and certain livestock.

CHAPTER 11

ORDERS OF PROTECTION

An Order of Protection is available for parties who are being stalked, harassed, or abused by their partner (physically, verbally, or sexually). It is available not only for romantic relationships (e.g., spouse, boyfriend/girlfriend), but also other family relationships (e.g., between a farmer landlord uncle and farmer tenant niece). Although the procedures for filing and defending against an order of protection vary from state to state, this chapter breaks down the general process.

FILING THE PETITION

The filing procedures themselves differ from state to state, so it is important to work with an attorney licensed in that jurisdiction. Litigants are encouraged to have a timeline prepared of all applicable events, including supporting documentation (e.g., text messages) to file along with the petition.

Some localities have domestic violence organizations that will help victims file petitions by leading them through the process. Many states have self-help centers to help those without attorneys file a petition against their abuser.

The name of the petition itself can vary from state to state. In some states, the petition is a Petition for an Order of Protection and in other states this may be called a Family Offense Petition. Typically, there is both a Petitioner and Respondent, but some states may refer to the parties as a Plaintiff and Defendant. If there is an ongoing divorce action, this matter may be consolidated into the matrimonial case for judicial economy.

SEEKING EMERGENCY RELIEF (IF APPLICABLE)

Usually, but not always, the second step is for the litigant to seek emergency relief from the court. This is referred to as an Emergency or Temporary Order of Protection and is usually for a few weeks or up to 30 days, until the initial court appearance.

This proceeding is typically *ex parte* (i.e., without the presence of the other side). Testimony is not usually taken at this court date; as a general rule, the determination of whether to grant the emergency order is done on the paper. The claimant should be in court in case the judge has questions. The Respondent/Defendant is then personally served by the police with the Emergency/Temporary Order of Protection, along with the underlying Petition.

HEARING ON PETITION FOR ORDER OF PROTECTION

There may be a series of court dates, but eventually a hearing date is set. This is an evidentiary hearing with both direct and cross examination. One can bring exhibits and supporting evidence. Depending on the time allotted by the court, cooperating witnesses may appear and testify.

Depending on the state, an Order of Protection may be granted for a period less than five years. This order usually includes a "stay away" of a certain radius (usually 500') and a no contact order. Ancillary relief may also be sought, such as restitution. The court has discretion to other relief, such as anger management courses, exclusive occupancy, support issues (e.g., spousal support or payment of household expenses), or children issues (e.g., parenting time, support). Depending on the jurisdiction, attorneys' fees may be sought. Please note that there can be carve-outs for exchange of children or communication about the children only.

ENSURING COMPLIANCE WITH PETITION

At the end of the day, an Order of Protection is just a piece of paper. The onus is on the Petitioner/Plaintiff to enforce its provisions. If the Respondent/Defendant has violated the terms of the Order of Protection, then the policy should be contacted immediately. Persons who have obtained an Order of Protection should always keep a copy of it on their person (e.g., in their purse), but also at their home and place of employment. Loved ones should be notified of the Order of Protection and, if appropriate, also have a copy of the Order of Protection.

CONSIDERATION OF EXTENSIONS

Depending on the state, an extension of the Order of Protection may be sought for good cause shown, such as violations of the Order of Protection or continued threats. This area of law varies significantly from state to state and with certain localities, so please seek a family lawyer nearby for information.

FINAL CONSIDERATIONS

Both parties to an Order of Protection should seek counsel to help them maneuver the process. Filing parties should consider safety when filing an Order of Protection, especially if that person lives with the alleged abuser. Persons defending against Orders of Protection should understand the inherent seriousness of the matter and potential impacts on employment in agriculture if an Order of Protection is issued against them. Terms of Orders of Protections, including emergency/interim/temporary orders, should be strictly followed by both parties.

CHAPTER 12

USE OF THIRD PARTIES WITH FINANCIAL

DISPUTES

Most divorces concerning farms, ranches, and food/agribusinesses have more complex financial issues than the average divorce. There are third parties that may assist you with this process such as appraisers, business evaluators, and Certified Divorce Financial Planners.

APPRAISERS

You can get almost anything appraised and in a farm divorce, you may need to. Depending on the assets of your farm or ranch, you may need to hire a farm equipment appraiser, who will need a detailed inventory list of all the equipment. There may be a need to appraise both residential and or commercial real estate and appraise livestock, including equine.

There are also specialized appraisers for antiques, art, and intellectual property. Actuaries can help ascertain marital portions of retirement assets.

BUSINESS EVALUATORS

A common mistake with farm and ranch divorces is that they believe that the business itself only has liquidation value, i.e., the farm or ranch is only worth the value of its assets. But this is usually untrue. A business evaluator will look at the last 5+ years of tax returns and financial data to ascertain the value of the business itself.

FORENSIC ACCOUNTANTS

If there are issues or confusion with the farm or ranch books, then a forensic accounting may be performed on the books. This can be an expensive and time-consuming process but may be necessary to ensure the accuracy of the data for valuation purposes.

CERTIFIED DIVORCE FINANCIAL PLANNERS

Certified Divorce Financial Planners or Financial Advisors can run an analysis of Settlement Offer A vs. Settlement Offer B. This can be useful when weighing options between longer term payment plan vs. short term payout in either direction.

CHAPTER 13

ALTERNATIVE DISPUTE RESOLUTION

Folks going through a divorce or separation should consider Alternative Dispute Resolution ("ADR") as a way to help resolve issues outside of the courtroom, in whole or part. Litigation can be expensive and resolving matters through the help of an ADR professional can be cheaper and faster. There are also other advantages of ADR including the preservation of the relationship, which may be especially important with some families.

Here are a few different forms of ADR which are applicable to divorce and separation including:

1. Mediation;
2. Arbitration;
3. Early Neutral Evaluation; and
4. Conciliation.

MEDIATION

Mediation is the most common form of ADR in a divorce. A mediator is there to facilitate a conversation between the two of you to discuss the applicable issues. A mediation session is usually between 1.5 to 2.5 hours for each session and it can sometimes take about 2 to 5 (or more) mediation sessions to reach a global settlement. The role of the mediator is not to provide you legal advice- that is the role of the attorneys.

ARBITRATION

Arbitration is akin to a trial where the arbitrator acts like a judge reviewing documents provided by both sides and making either a binding or non-binding decision for the two of you. In Illinois, an arbitrator can only be used for economic decisions for the divorce and can never be used for determining issues of child custody and visitation.

EARLY NEUTRAL EVALUATION

Early Neutral Evaluation is a growing but more rare form of ADR. Like an arbitrator, a neutral evaluator is an experienced professional who reviews arguments and documents from each party. The neutral evaluator gives an opinion on what he/she believes an experienced jurist would decide. This can be particularly helpful if the parties are at an impasse.

CONCILIATION

Conciliation is short for reconciliation. The role of the conciliator is to try to help the couple reconcile. In some situation, the conciliator is also a mediator. Once reconciliation is futile, then the conversation may shift to divorce or separation.

COLLABORATIVE DIVORCE

Please note that a collaborative divorce is a different model. In this form of ADR, a mediator is used while both parties are represented by their own consulting attorney. Both parties agree in writing that if either goes to court that they will go get new attorneys. Other professionals are sometimes used in this model such as accountants, financial advisors, and therapists.

CHAPTER 14

USE OF OTHER PROFESSIONALS

Not only should those involved in farm and ranch divorces consider appraisers and financial experts, but there are other types of professionals that can be useful in your family's transition. Like farm estate and succession planning, farm families should consider a team approach to divorce and separation. After all, Divorce is one of the Big D's that harms multi-generational farm families.

THERAPISTS

Especially if children are involved, consider using a therapist to aid in the transition. Depending on the professional, this therapist may aid in family therapy to help parents with co-parenting and communication skills. They can even work with each spouse and the children in individual and or joint session. It is suggested to take the therapist's lead in this regard on what is best for your family. As a reminder, many therapists take health insurance so be sure so investigate this option.

PARENT COORDINATORS

Parent coordinators are best for high conflict families. They are typically therapists and can be court ordered in limited situations. The parent coordinator can work with families much like an arbitrator making decisions for the parents when they are at an impasse. This is a much-preferred option as opposed to going to court each time the parents are in a disagreement on a major decision involving health, education, religion, or extracurricular activities or in dispute about parenting time issues such an exchange concerns and school breaks.

FINANCIAL ADVISORS

It is not uncommon in a divorce or separation for one or both people to decide to obtain a new financial advisor. It is a great chance to take advantage of this fresh start to ensure your financial advisor is knowledgeable to help you navigate your divorce and separation. There are some financial advisors who have received advance training in this area such as Certified Divorce Financial Planners (check on name).

ACCOUNTANTS

Similarly, as with financial advisors, it is not uncommon for folks to obtain their own accountant during this transition. Be sure this accountant understands the unique agriculture concerns of your farm family.

REAL ESTATE BROKERS

Residential and or commercial real estate brokers may be used to sell the marital residence, commercial farm, or ranch land or other property pursuant to a divorce settlement agreement. Those in need should be cognizant of the experience of the real estate brokers with farm and ranch families.

INSURANCE BROKER

Hopefully, your farm or ranch family already has a relationship with an insurance broker. Perhaps one person may choose to obtain his or her own broker. Insurance can be negotiated in divorces in several different scenarios including security for spousal maintenance and or child support (sometimes including post-secondary education), buy-sell agreements with farm families, security for debt in a farming or ranch operation, etc.

DIVORCE COACHES

Scientifically, your ability to focus and concentrate becomes more difficult when someone is experiencing trauma or significant stress. A divorce coach can help someone gather up and organize financial documents needed for the attorney, attend meetings and court appearances with clients, and coach him or her on how to communicate with their children and or soon-to-be-ex spouse to better maneuver the divorce or separation.

PARENTING CLASSES

Depending on your state or locality, a parenting class may be required by the courts. For example, in Illinois parties with minor children must take a Children's First class in their county unless otherwise ordered by the court. In New York, judges have discretion whether to order a parenting class to one or both parties. Parties going through a divorce or separation should speak to their attorney to understand what is required but also investigate voluntary options.

These classes can be useful discussing issues such as communication with your children about the divorce or separation and to not communicate with the other parent (especially about money) via the children. These parenting classes are invaluable to help families navigate this transition and conflict.

PARENTING COACHES

To compliment the parenting classes, in some cases, parents opt to hire private parenting coaches to help them maneuver among the different states of parenthood, especially while going through a divorce. These parenting coaches are usually done separately but can also be in joint session.

LIFE COACHES

Life coaches are oftentimes confused with therapists, but they serve unique purposes. Life coaches are more goal centered helping clients meet those rocks by keeping them on track and accountable. For example, a life coach (or career coach) may be helpful to help someone get a job after significant time out of the workforce.

HEALTH COACHES

It is not uncommon for people to shift priorities after a divorce or separation to focusing on self-improvement and their health. If this is you, health coaches can help keep people accountable towards their goals, even if it is simply drinking more water or eating more fresh farm fruits and veggies.

DATING COACHES

Dating should be done cautiously during and after a divorce and separation, oftentimes with the guidance of a therapist to decide when is the best time to start dating again; however, there is a coach for everything, including helping one get out there again and navigate dating again. If you live in a rural community, many of these dating coaches are located in more urban areas but speak to clients via Skype and telephone.

FINANCIAL ORGANIZER

It is not uncommon for one person in a marriage to manage monies of the family. This poses a challenge for the person who is not the money manager of the family as he/she is learning about paying bills, budgeting, and balancing a checkbook for the first time in years. A financial organizer is different than the Financial Advisor and helps people learn to manage cash flow, paying bills, and coaching them to use programs such as Quicken, Mint, or EveryDollar.

MEDIATOR

Mediation and other forms of ADR are found in another chapter but it is worth noting briefly here. It cannot be stressed enough how important it is for farm and ranch families to consider mediation to help resolve children and or economic issues. Mediators are a neutral third party to help facilitate a conversation between the parties.

Mediation can be especially helpful for complex farm and ranch divorces. It is naive to believe that this will be resolved in one mediation session. As a general rule, it can take two to five mediation sessions (about two to three hours for each session) to resolve all global issues. It can take more if there are complex parenting issues or financial issues, which are oftentimes prevalent in farm and ranch divorces.

ADDITIONAL RESOURCES

Cari B. Rincker et al., ONWARD AND UPWARD: GUIDE FOR GETTING THROUGH NEW YORK DIVORCE AND FAMILY LAW ISSUES (2015) available at https://www.amazon.com/Onward-Upward-Getting-Through-Divorce/dp/0692556540

Cari B. Rincker, "I'm Talking About the Big D and a I Don't Mean Dallas" (May 2019), available at https://www.slideshare.net/rinckerlaw/im-talking-about-the-big-d-family-law-issues-in-agriculture

American Academy of Matrimonial Lawyers, Online Book store, available at https://aaml.org/store/ListProducts.aspx?catid=704530

ABOUT THE AUTHOR

Cari B. Rincker is the principal attorney at Rincker Law, PLLC, a national law firm concentrating in food and agriculture law. Cari is licensed to practice law in Illinois, New York, New Jersey, Connecticut and the District of Columbia.

Cari grew up on a Simmental farm in Shelbyville, Illinois showing cattle through 4-H and FFA and is still involved in her family's beef cattle operation. Cari enjoys judging county and state fair livestock shows in her free time. She is also an adjunct professor at Vermont Law School and the University of Illinois. She too is a past-adjunct professor at New York University, Steinhardt School of Education, Department of Nutrition, Food Studies and Public Health.

Cari is a Distinguished Alumni from Lake Land College in Mattoon, Illinois where she obtained her Associate in Science in Agriculture. She went on to receive her Bachelors in Science in Animal Science from Texas A & M University where she also become a member of the All-American Livestock Judging Team. In 2012, Cari received an Outstanding Early Career Award from Texas A & M University, College of Agriculture and Life Sciences.

Under the supervision of Dr. Larry Berger, Cari received her Masters of Science in Ruminant Nutrition from the University of Illinois where her thesis research was focused in the area of beef feedlot nutrition and genetics. Cari obtained her Juris Doctor with Certificates in Environmental Law and International Law from Pace University, School of Law in White Plains, New York.

Before starting Rincker Law, PLLC, Cari was an associate with Budd-Falen Law Offices, LLC in Cheyenne, Wyoming, a consultant with the Food & Agriculture Organization ("FAO") of the United Nations ("UN") in Rome, Italy, and a junior delegate with the Permanent Mission of the Marshall Islands to the UN in New York, New York. She was elected as the "Best Agriculture Lawyer" in the 2011 and 2012 Best of Barns Competition and was awarded the "Excellence in Agriculture" Award in the Private Practice Division with the American Agriculture Law Association.

Cari has two offices in Illinois both in downtown Champaign and Shelbyville, Illinois (her hometown). Her New York office is located in Midtown Manhattan in New York City. You can contact

Cari at cari@rinckerlaw.com.

You can subscribe to her Food, Farm, & Family Law Blog at www.rinckerlaw.com/blog or follow her on Twitter @RinckerLaw or @CariRincker. Cari also has a YouTube Channel at www.youtube.com/caririncker and a podcast with Purdue University call Ag Law Today that is available on iTunes, YouTube and Purdue Extension Education's Website.

SPEAKING ENGAGEMENTS

Have Cari Speak At Your Next
Food or Agriculture Event!

Cari B. Rincker is a prolific writer and recognized speaker on a myriad of food and agriculture law topics. She is available to speak on food and agriculture law topics at your next event in Illinois, New York or other places across the country or the world.

Her speaking engagements include: Animal Agriculture Alliance Annual Stakeholders Summit, New York Farm Bureau Animal Welfare Conference, New York Farm Bureau Young Farmers' and Ranchers' Conference, Texas Bar CLE, Ohio Agriculture Law Symposium, North Carolina Agriculture Law Conference, American Agriculture Law Association's Annual Meeting, American Bar Association, New York Agri-Women Annual Meeting, Bar Association for the City of New York, American Cattlewomen National Beef Speakers Bureau, Pace Law School, Lawline, New York 4-H, Cornell Cooperative Extension, National Agriculture Law Center, Lawline, etc.

To book Cari for your next Illinois event, either call (217) 531-2179 or write Cari via email at cari@rinckerlaw.com, facsimile (212) 202-6077, or via U.S. mail at 301 N. Neil Street, Suite 400, Champaign, IL 61820, with the following information:

- Name of the event,
- Date, time, and location of the engagement,
- Suggested food and agriculture law topics,
- Anticipated audience,
- Technology available for the event,
- Deadline for materials, and
- Transportation costs and honorarium.

In this post COVID-19 world, Cari is also proficient in videoconference technology such a Zoom, GoToMeeting and Skype. She has been broadcasted live on YouTube speaking on entrepreneurial and agriculture issues and is able to speak online at your next virtual event.

Form to Book Cari at Next Event

Your Name:	
Your Organization:	
Your Contact Info: (Address, Phone, Email)	
Name of the Event:	
Date(s) of the Event:	
Location of Event:	
Suggested Topic(s):	
Length of Presentation:	
Audience:	
Anticipated Deadline for Materials:	
Transportation Costs/ Honorarium:	

Email to cari@rinckerlaw.com or fax to (212) 202-6077.